United States Government Accountability Office

Report to Congressional Requesters

I0426149

April 2012

EXPORT CONTROLS

U.S. Agencies Need to Assess Control List Reform's Impact on Compliance Activities

G A O
Accountability * Integrity * Reliability

GAO-12-613

G A O
Accountability * Integrity * Reliability

Highlights

Highlights of GAO-12-613, a report to congressional requesters

EXPORT CONTROLS

U.S. Agencies Need to Assess Control List Reform's Impact on Compliance Activities

Why GAO Did This Study

To protect its national security and commercial interests, the United States has implemented an export control system to limit sensitive technologies from falling into the wrong hands. The Department of State regulates U.S. defense exports and the Department of Commerce regulates dual-use exports that have commercial and military applications. Each agency uses a separate control list of items that may require a license to export. Agencies use compliance activities to prevent the diversion or misuse of exported items against U.S. interests or allies. Misuse can occur through illicit transshipment, the diversion of items from their origin through an intermediary country to an unauthorized destination. In 2010, the President announced reforms to the export control system.

This review examines (1) agencies' compliance activities to address transshipment risk and (2) the extent to which U.S. agencies assessed the impact of export control reforms on the resource needs for compliance activities. GAO analyzed U.S. licensing data for 13 transshipment countries and visited Hong Kong, Singapore, and the United Arab Emirates.

What GAO Recommends

GAO recommends that Commerce and State should assess the potential impact of control list reforms on the resource needs of their compliance activities. Commerce and State concurred with GAO's recommendation.

View GAO-12-613. For more information, contact Thomas Melito at (202) 512-9601 or melitot@gao.gov.

What GAO Found

U.S. agencies engaged in export controls use various compliance activities to prevent the diversion or misuse of exported items against U.S. interests or allies and reduce illicit transshipment risk. Compliance activities include (1) vetting transactions prior to export, (2) analyzing shipping data and monitoring the end use of items, and (3) educating companies and foreign governments about illicit transshipment risks. To vet transactions, agencies review license applications for the export of controlled items, consult multiple lists of entities known or suspected of violating export control laws or regulations, and screen foreign end users to determine their eligibility to receive items without a license. Agencies also review shipping records to identify patterns of abuse and to plan end-use checks—visiting foreign companies to verify the approved use and location of exported items on both licensed items and those eligible for export without a license. From 2008 to 2010, Commerce conducted 56 percent of its end-use checks on unlicensed exports. In the 13 transshipment countries, unlicensed exports accounted for about 94 percent of unfavorable end-use check determinations, which indicates that the end use or end user of an export were not appropriate. For example, some unlicensed items transshipped illicitly to Iran through Hong Kong were used to build improvised explosive devices used against Coalition troops in Iraq. When an unfavorable determination is made, the Department of Commerce (Commerce) or Department of State (State) may take further action, such as denying a license or referring involved entities to enforcement agencies for investigation and possible penalties. To educate U.S. companies and foreign governments about illicit transshipment risks, Commerce and State review the internal controls of companies' compliance programs; conduct outreach to U.S. companies to inform exporters of their responsibilities to comply with export control laws and regulations; and provide training to foreign governments.

Agencies have not fully assessed the potential impact that control list reforms may pose for the resource needs of their compliance activities. Agencies estimate that Commerce will receive between 16,000 and 30,000 additional license applications as a result of proposed reforms to move less sensitive items from State to Commerce. Agency documents state that this step would allow them to focus resources on items most critical to national security and may make compliance easier for exporters because Commerce imposes fewer requirements than State's controls. However, Commerce has not assessed the impact this added responsibility would have on its end-use check resource needs. Also, under the reforms, fewer items may require export licenses, thereby reducing uncertainty as to whether export sales will be approved. Some agency officials suggested potential risks, such as an increased need for more end-use checks and the loss of information from reviewing exports through the licensing process prior to export. The agencies have not yet assessed the impact of these potential risks on their resource needs.

Contents

Tables

Figures

Abbreviations

BIS	Bureau of Industry and Security
CCL	Commerce Control List
DDTC	Directorate of Defense Trade Controls
DOD	Department of Defense
EAR	Export Administration Regulations
ECO	Export Control Officer
EXBS	Export Controls and Border Security
OFAC	Office of Foreign Assets Control
PSV	post-shipment verification
SDN	Specially Designated Nationals
STA	Strategic Trade Authorization
UAE	United Arab Emirates
USML	U.S. Munitions List
VEU	Validated End-User
WMD	weapons of mass destruction

United States Government Accountability Office
Washington, DC 20548

April 23, 2012

The Honorable Susan M. Collins
Ranking Member
Committee on Homeland Security
 and Governmental Affairs
United States Senate

The Honorable Jon Kyl
Ranking Member
Subcommittee on Crime and Terrorism
Committee on the Judiciary
United States Senate

To further its national security and economic interests, the United States controls the export of sensitive defense and dual-use items (having both commercial and military applications) to foreign governments and commercial entities. Such items can range from sophisticated technology designed for military use, such as F-15 aircraft, to unsophisticated and commonly available electronic switches that have ultimately been used in improvised explosive devices by terrorists in Iraq and Afghanistan. The U.S. government seeks to limit the risk of sensitive items falling into the wrong hands, while allowing legitimate trade to occur and uses the export control system to balance these U.S. interests. Multiple federal agencies administer the laws, regulations, and processes that make up the regulatory compliance and enforcement framework governing the export control system. Primarily, the Department of State (State) regulates defense exports, and the Department of Commerce (Commerce) regulates dual-use exports.[1] Each agency maintains a separate list of items to be controlled and exported with a license after government review, or without a license under designated exceptions.

The U.S. government also conducts activities to encourage compliance with its export control laws and to prevent the diversion or misuse of

---

[1]In addition, the Department of Defense (DOD) provides input on which items should be controlled by either State or Commerce and conducts technical and national security reviews of export license applications submitted by exporters to either State or Commerce.

exported items against U.S. interests or allies.[2] Compliance activities include reviewing export license applications to decide whether to approve or deny them, visiting foreign companies to verify the approved use and location of exported items—referred to as end-use checks—and conducting courses for exporters—called outreach—to inform them of their responsibilities to comply with export control laws and regulations. Of particular concern to the agencies conducting compliance efforts is illicit transshipment of items—the transfer of merchandise from its place of origin through an intermediary country—to an unauthorized final destination such as Iran.[3] Illicit transshipment challenges compliance efforts because it poses a significant risk to the safe transfer of sensitive U.S. technologies to authorized end users.

Our reports to Congress and testimony at congressional hearings have highlighted the need for export control reform. We have called for, among other things, a strategic reexamination of existing programs within the U.S. export control system to identify needed changes and ensure the advancement of U.S. interests. In 2010, the United States announced a fundamental reform of its export control system, by proposing, among other things, to reduce the numbers and types of items requiring government review and licensing before export. Members of Congress raised concerns that, absent efforts to first address compliance and enforcement shortfalls, reform of the system could exacerbate current weaknesses, including the risk of illicit transshipment.

In this review, we (1) examined how U.S. agencies use compliance activities to address the risk of illicit transshipment and (2) analyzed the extent to which U.S. agencies assessed the impact of the export control reform on the resource needs of compliance activities. This is the fourth in a series of four reports we have issued on this subject since November

---

[2]"Diversion" refers to the transfer or release, directly or indirectly, of a good, service, or technology to an end user or an intermediary that is not an authorized recipient of the good, service, or technology.

[3]The U.S. government has no agreed-upon definition of transshipment. However, the Census Bureau proposed a definition stating that "transshipment" refers to the transfer of merchandise from the country or countries of origin through an intermediary country or countries to the country of destination. We use that definition for the purposes of this report. Transshipment is one type of reexport, according to Commerce, whose regulations define reexport as the shipment or transmission of an item subject to the Export Administration Regulations from one foreign country to another. According to Commerce, diversion can occur through transshipment.

2010. Our first report identified the extent to which agencies' actions and the proposed export control framework addressed findings in our previous reports in the areas of export control lists, licensing, enforcement, and information technology.[4] Our second report, issued on March 14, 2012, was a version of this report containing information designated "For Official Use Only." Our third report, issued on March 27, 2012, covered the enforcement of U.S. export controls in light of the Export Control Reform Initiative.[5]

To address the two objectives of this review, we analyzed licensing, end-use monitoring, and other data from Commerce, State, and the Department of the Treasury (Treasury) for 13 transshipment countries and locations.[6] We also drew a random, nongeneralizable sample of 56 Commerce end-use checks and 21 State end-use checks to determine how results from those activities were incorporated into other compliance activities. We identified export control compliance activities that Commerce, State, and Treasury conduct to encourage compliance with export control laws and to prevent the diversion or misuse of exported items against U.S. allies or interests. We identified these compliance activities through interviews with agency officials and review of documentation. Appendix II lists and describes the eight compliance activities that we reviewed. We met with U.S. officials of Commerce, the DOD, State, and Treasury, and representatives of companies in Washington, D.C., and with U.S. embassy and foreign government officials in Hong Kong, Singapore, and the United Arab Emirates (UAE). We reviewed documentation on agency actions taken to encourage

---

[4]GAO, *Export Controls: Agency Actions and Proposed Reform Initiatives May Address Previously Identified Weaknesses, but Challenges Remain,* GAO-11-135R (Washington, D.C.: Nov. 16, 2010).

[5]GAO, *Export Controls: Proposed Reforms Create Opportunities to Address Enforcement Challenges,* GAO-12-246 (Washington, D.C.: Mar. 27, 2012).

[6]For the purpose of this report, we designated as transshipment countries Canada, China, Cyprus, Hong Kong (a special administrative region of China), Indonesia, Jordan, Malaysia, Malta, Philippines, Singapore, Taiwan, Thailand, and UAE. We generated this list of 13 transshipment countries by reviewing prior GAO work on transshipment and diversion; congressional testimony; countries with entities on the Entity List or Unverified List; input from State and Commerce; lists of the busiest transshipment ports worldwide; and those countries where a Commerce Export Control Officer has been stationed. We refer to Hong Kong and Taiwan as transshipment "countries" only for the purposes of this report. None of the agencies we contacted maintains a comparable list of transshipment countries.

compliance actions and interviewed U.S. government officials, including representatives of Commerce's Bureau of Industry and Security (BIS); DOD's Defense Technology Security Administration; State's Directorate of Defense Trade Controls (DDTC); and Treasury's Office of Foreign Assets Control (OFAC). We also spoke with export control reform task force members and reviewed recent White House press releases on the export reform initiatives. U.S. agencies engage in a variety of activities intended to foster compliance with U.S. export control law and regulations, and other activities to enforce these laws and exact penalties for violating them. We did not review enforcement activities that address investigations, civil and criminal penalties, seizures, indictments, prosecutions, or convictions as our third report addressed these activities. Commerce provided us with transshipment-related information that it controls as being "For Official Use Only." We have not included that information in this report but have instead incorporated it into a "For Official Use Only" report that is not publicly available. Appendix I discusses our scope and methodology in more detail.

We conducted this performance audit from August 2010 to April 2012 in accordance with generally accepted government auditing standards. These standards require that we plan and perform the audit to obtain sufficient, appropriate evidence to provide a reasonable basis for our findings and conclusions based on our audit objectives. We believe that the evidence obtained provides a reasonable basis for our findings and conclusions based on our audit objectives.

Background

Export Control System

The current U.S. export control system seeks to limit sensitive items from falling into the wrong hands and, at the same time, allow legitimate trade to occur. The export control system is governed by a complex set of laws, regulations, and processes and multiple federal agencies administer its regulatory framework and ensure compliance. State and Commerce each have a role in U.S. export licensing. Generally, exporters may submit a license application to State if their items are controlled on the U.S. Munitions List (USML) or to Commerce if their items are controlled on the Commerce Control List (CCL) to receive export approval. Exemptions are permitted under various circumstances, such as allowing for the export of certain items to Canada without a license. Even though many dual-use items do not require a license for export to most destinations, they are still subject to U.S. export control laws. All items subject to the Export

Administration Regulations (EAR), whether or not on the CCL, require exporters to comply with the EAR.[7] As part of the application review process, State and Commerce consult with other agencies, including DOD. Exporters require a license for most arms exports. In 2010, Commerce processed 21,660 export licenses, and State processed 82,937 export licenses.[8] Additionally, offices within State, Commerce, Treasury, and the Departments of Homeland Security and Justice conduct compliance activities to identify potential violations or prevent them before they occur; they also conduct export control enforcement activities to identify and penalize violations after they occur. When compliance activities, such as end-use checks, result in unfavorable determinations, Commerce or State may take further action, such as denying a license or referring involved entities to enforcement agencies for investigation and possible penalties. Enforcement also strives to prevent or deter the illegal export of defense and dual–use items, such as controlled components that were shipped to countries like Iran, which were later found in weapons and devices used against U.S. forces in Iraq. Export control enforcement activities include inspecting items to be exported, investigating potential export control violations, and pursuing and imposing criminal and administrative penalties against violators.

The imposition of economic sanctions has been a long-standing tool for addressing a range of national security threats. As of February 2012, OFAC maintains primary responsibility for administering more than 20 separate sanctions programs. These sanctions programs include (1) country-based programs that apply sanctions to an entire country—such as Iran, or Sudan; and (2) targeted, list-based programs that address individuals or entities engaged in specific types of activities such as

---

[7]For items controlled by Commerce, exporters are to determine whether a license is required or one of the licensing exceptions permissible under the EAR is applicable. Commerce may require a license for an export based on a variety of reasons, including limiting the proliferation of chemical, biological weapons and the country of destination. A license exception, as opposed to a license requirement, is an authorization that allows an exporter to export or reexport without a license, under stated conditions, items subject to the EAR, which would otherwise require a license. If an item is not listed on the control list but is subject to the EAR, it falls into a category known as EAR99. State refers to the eligibility of exports of items on the USML without a license under certain conditions as exemptions.

[8]This State number represents all arms export license processed by DDTC, which include applications for the export of arms and agreements between U.S. industry and foreign entities to provide technical assistance or manufacturing capability.

terrorism, proliferation of weapons of mass destruction (WMD), or narcotics trafficking. For example, according to Treasury officials, they use the authorities under the International Emergency Economic Powers Act and Executive Order 13224 to designate those who provide support to terrorists, freezing any assets they have under U.S. jurisdiction and preventing U.S. persons from doing business with them.[9]

Export Control Reform Initiative

In August 2009, the President announced that he was directing a comprehensive review of the U.S. export control system. This review found that the U.S. export control system has a complicated structure with multiple agencies and control lists, which has led to jurisdictional confusion and hindered the ability of allies to cooperate with U.S. forces. In April 2010, the administration announced a reform framework that would create an export control system that is more effective, transparent, and predictable by creating a single control list, licensing agency, enforcement agency, and information technology system for licensing. The administration also found that licensing procedures and conditions are not consolidated or uniform across agencies, with various agencies monitoring and enforcing export controls.[10] The current process relies on separate information systems, some of which are paper-based, which are not accessible to all agencies involved.

Our past work has highlighted the need for export control reform through reports to Congress and testimony at congressional hearings. Over the last decade, GAO has made a number of key findings and recommendations directed to State, Commerce, DOD, Homeland Security, Justice, and Treasury, to improve the U.S. export control system.[11] Some of the issues we identified include a lack of systematic assessments, poor interagency coordination, and inefficiencies in the license application process.

---

[9]Under the authority provided by the International Emergency Economic Powers Act (50 U.S.C. §§1701 et seq.), the President has continued the EAR in effect through Executive Order No. 13222 of August 17, 2001 (3 C.F.R., 2001 Comp. p. 738 (2002)), as extended most recently by Notice of August 12, 2011, 76 *Fed. Reg*, 50661.

[10]In 2007, GAO designated the programs that identify and protect technologies critical to U.S. national security interests as a high-risk area. GAO has maintained its designation. See GAO, *High-Risk Series: An Update,* GAO-07-310 (Washington, D.C.: January 2007); and *High Risk Series: An Update,* GAO-11-278 (Washington, D.C.: February 2011).

[11]A list of Related GAO Products appears at the end of this report.

The administration plans to begin implementing export control reforms through interim changes that can be carried out by regulation or executive order. Reforms requiring legislative action—creation of a single licensing agency, control list, and enforcement agency—will come last and had not been proposed as of March 2012. As of February 2012, the administration has taken steps to implement export control reform including proposing regulations to move controlled export items from the USML to the CCL, and clarifying which items pertain to each list, and establishing an Export Enforcement Coordination Center by executive order.[12]

Transshipment and Diversion

In July 2010, a senior State official testified that transshipment hubs (i.e., countries or areas that function as major hubs for the legitimate trading and shipment of cargo) with weak controls on imports, exports, and reexports represent an important vulnerability to efforts to prevent illicit proliferation-related trade. Our previous work identified cases of illicit transshipment involving parties in UAE, Singapore, and Malaysia.[13] As congressional attention focused on transshipment, members also raised concerns about the resources needed for compliance activities, domestically and overseas. For example, in the same July 2010 hearing, a member expressed concern that only one Commerce individual was stationed in the UAE to conduct end-use checks for dual-use exports.[14] According to U.S. officials, Iran has obtained U.S. military and dual-use goods that have been illegally transshipped by firms and individuals through locations in numerous countries, including the UAE, Malaysia, and Singapore. The goods included components for U.S.-built fighter aircraft, electronics, and specialized metals. To address the problem, U.S.

---

[12]See Exec. Order No. 13558, 75 *Fed. Reg.* 69, 573 (Nov. 15, 2010).

[13]GAO, *Iran Sanctions: Complete and Timely Licensing Data Needed to Strengthen Enforcement of Export Restrictions*, GAO-10-375 (Washington, D.C.: Mar. 4, 2010).

[14]End-use checks are conducted to determine the bona fides of the transaction and the end user, and to ensure that an exported item is being used in accordance with U.S. export control regulations and the terms of the export license. Commerce determines that end-use checks had favorable, unfavorable, or limited and nonconclusive results. A check is favorable when it can confirm the end use and end user of an export are appropriate. An unfavorable determination means that Commerce considers the end user to be unreliable. Nonconclusive determinations result when Commerce cannot determine the reliability of the end user. For example, if Commerce is unable to conduct a site visit. A limited result means that the individual conducting the check provided incomplete information or did not follow Commerce guidance in carrying out the check.

agencies have conducted undercover investigations to detect Iranian procurement networks, prosecuted criminal cases against at least 30 firms and individuals for transshipping or attempting to transship goods to Iran, and provided export control training and support to the UAE and other countries.

Compliance Activities Address Illicit Transshipment Risk in Three Areas

U.S. agencies engaged in export controls use multiple compliance activities to reduce illicit transshipment risk. These activities include (1) vetting transactions prior to export by screening applications against four categories of lists of parties of concern, among other steps, (2) analyzing shipping data and monitoring end use of items, and (3) educating companies and foreign governments about the risks of illicit transshipment, although State's outreach efforts have been largely inactive since 2008.

U.S. Agencies Vet Transactions Prior to Export

To address illicit transshipment risks, agencies vet parties to transactions prior to export in three ways. First, agencies examine license applications to assess the transaction. Second, they vet individual parties to the transaction by, for example, confirming their credentials before issuing a license (a prelicense check). Third, agencies screen applicants to identify trusted end users for the Validated End-User (VEU) program.

License Application Review Vets Transactions Prior to Export

When deciding to approve or deny an export license application, Commerce and State evaluate it against several factors, including an assessment of all parties to the transaction and how the recipient plans to use the item. Commerce factors the risk of illicit transshipment into the license application review process through a risk assessment tool that assigns a weighted score to an application, based on the level of concern associated with the listed party, country, product, and exporter. A high score may prompt further investigation and an end-use check by Commerce or embassy officials. In technical comments on a draft of this report, Commerce stated that the risk assessment tool would affect the license review process only when Commerce determined that a prelicense check would be necessary. In those cases, Commerce incorporates transshipment risk in the license application review process by dividing countries into three categories of risk, with the third category including countries identified as transshipment points. Commerce's list of highest risk countries includes 7 of the 13 transshipment countries in our review. For fiscal years 2008 through 2010, Commerce reviewed 63,304 license applications worldwide, 19,693 (31 percent) of which were for exports to the 13 transshipment countries we identified. It approved 84 percent of license applications for these transshipment countries, denied 1 percent, and returned 15 percent of the applications to exporters without taking action on them.[15] Appendix III contains additional information on the number of license applications that Commerce and State reviewed for the 13 transshipment countries between fiscal years 2008 and 2010.

State conducts a case-by-case review of export license applications against established criteria or "warning flags" for determining potential risk of exporting USML items to foreign recipients. As part of the license review process, State may conduct a prelicense end-use check to provide more information on the transaction before it acts on the license application. State's guidance on conducting end-use checks (known as Blue Lantern monitoring) identifies three broad categories that may trigger an end-use check, including whether there are indicators for transshipment through multiple countries or companies.[16] For fiscal years 2008 through 2010, State reviewed 164,998 license applications worldwide and 28,550 for exports to the 13 transshipment countries (17 percent of all applications).[17] It approved 86 percent of license applications for these countries,[18] denied 1 percent, returned without action 13 percent, and suspended or revoked 1 percent of preexisting licenses.[19]

Treasury does not review licenses for the 13 transshipment countries because none of these countries is an embargoed or sanctioned country.

---

[15]A licensing agency may return an export license application without action because the application lacked needed information or the applicant withdrew the application, among other reasons.

[16]Blue Lantern end-use monitoring entails the prelicense, postlicense, or postshipment inquiries or "checks" undertaken to verify the legitimacy of a transaction and to provide "reasonable assurance" that the recipient complies with the requirements imposed by the U.S. government with respect to use, transfers, and security of defense articles and defense services; and that such articles and services are being used for the purposes for which they were provided.

[17]For the purpose of this report, we reviewed licenses for permanent export. State also authorizes temporary exports and technical data.

[18]Approved license applications include those that were approved with provisos, such as those specifying how items can be used and by whom.

[19]Suspending a license temporarily removes the privilege of exporting, while revoking a license annuls it and rescinds the authority to export.

However, it assesses illicit transshipment risk when it licenses goods to several destinations, such as Iran and Sudan, in its administration of U.S. embargoes and sanctions. According to Treasury officials, OFAC screens end users in the license review process against the sanctions lists it administers because it assesses the risk of illicit transshipment or of reexport when placing individuals on these lists.

Agencies Screen Applications against Four Categories of Lists of Parties of Concern

Commerce, State, and Treasury each maintain several screening lists that inform the licensing process by providing information on entities of concern to licensing officers and the public. These lists encompass a range of designations including those related to proliferation of WMD, terrorism, and actions contrary to U.S. national security and foreign policy interests. We reviewed four categories of lists outlined in table 1 below.[20]

Table 1: Categories and Lists of Entities of Concern

Category	List	Agency	Description
Additional Licensing Requirements	Entity List	Commerce	List of parties that are subject to specific license requirements for the export, reexport, and/or in country transfer of specified items. Parties on this list are subject to licensing requirements.
Unverified Parties	Unverified List	Commerce	List of persons in foreign countries who were parties to past export transactions where prelicense checks or postshipment verifications could not be conducted for reasons outside the control of the U.S. government.
Prohibited and Sanctioned Parties	Specially Designated Nationals List	Treasury	List of blocked persons, blocked vessels, specially designated nationals, specially designated terrorists, specially designated global terrorists, foreign terrorist organizations, and specially designated narcotics traffickers whose assets are blocked and U.S. persons are generally prohibited from dealing with them.
	Nonproliferation Sanctions List	State	List of parties that have been sanctioned under various statutes, designed to combat the proliferation of WMD.

---

[20]Commerce officials also suggested that the public screen parties against the Denied Persons List and the AECA Debarred List. For the purposes of this report, we have classified these activities as enforcement rather than compliance activities.

Category	List	Agency	Description
Internal Watch Lists	Watch List – State	State	List of parties whose association with an export license application indicates a need for closer examination by licensing officers.
	Watch List – Commerce	Commerce	List of individuals and companies that Commerce has determined warrant increased scrutiny for export licensing purposes, including those companies that receive unfavorable end-use checks.

Source: GAO analysis of agency documents.

- *Entity List:* Commerce's considerations for additions to the Entity List include the end use of allegedly transshipped items. For example, on October 31, 2011, the End-User Review Committee added a firm located in Hong Kong and Singapore for diverting U.S.-origin items from Hong Kong to Iran.[21] The diversion was part of the efforts of a larger procurement network that arranged for the transshipment of radio frequency modules from Singapore to Iran for use in improvised explosive devices found in Iraq. Placement of an individual's name on the Entity List notifies exporters of a potential licensing requirement or a ban on exports. In August 2008, Commerce expanded criteria for addition to the Entity List to allow an entity to be placed on the list if there is reasonable cause to believe, based on specific and articulable facts, that the entity has been involved, is involved, or poses a significant risk of becoming involved in activities that are contrary to the national security or foreign policy interests of the United States. As of December 2010, at least 56 percent of the 359 entities on the Entity List[22] were from the 13 transshipment countries in our review.

- *Unverified List:* The Commerce Unverified List is a public list that includes the names and countries of foreign entities that were parties to transactions for which Commerce could not conduct a prelicense check or postshipment verification (PSV) due to factors outside of U.S. government control. The list informs the licensing process by providing exporters with information about entities of concern. For example, we determined that, of the 36 persons or entities currently

---

[21]The End-User Review Committee, composed of representatives of the Departments of State, Defense, Energy, and Commerce, and other agencies, as appropriate, is responsible for placing entities on the Entity List based on evidence that the entities pose a significant risk of involvement in activities contrary to U.S. national security or foreign policy interests. Commerce chairs the End-User Review Committee.

[22]In our analysis of the Entity List, we included entities and their subordinates and aliases in our calculations.

on the Unverified List, 78 percent are from the 13 transshipment countries we reviewed. When Commerce established the Unverified List in 2002, it advised exporters that the participation of a person on this list in any proposed transaction would raise a "red flag" for exporters under established guidance. Commerce stopped updating the Unverified List after it expanded the scope of the Entity List in August 2008 and is considering eliminating the Unverified List in 2012. Commerce officials said that they will review the Unverified List and assess the 36 entities currently on it against criteria for inclusion on the Entity List, transferring them, if warranted, on a case-by-case basis. Commerce will monitor the entities that are not transferred through its internal Watch List.

- *State and Treasury Sanctions Lists:* State and Treasury publish lists of individuals sanctioned under various statutes for activities relating to concerns ranging from nonproliferation to drug enforcement. Treasury officials indicated that both direct exports and transshipments from the United States to a sanctioned entity or to an embargoed country without authorization constitute diversion and are thus violations. For example, in December 2008, Treasury sanctioned an Iranian shipping line for facilitating the transport of cargo and employing deceptive shipping practices to advance Iran's nuclear and missile programs. Additionally, Treasury designated the company's subsidiaries in four transshipment countries—China, Malta, Singapore, and UAE. Of the 4,929 designations on the Specially Designated Nationals (SDN) list, 167 were from the 13 transshipment countries.[23]

- *State and Commerce Watch Lists:* State and Commerce screen parties named in a license application against internal Watch Lists, which include participants added because of illicit transshipment risk. Specifically, Commerce and State both add names of entities identified through unfavorable end-use checks, including names of

---

[23]The 167 entities designated on the SDN list from the 13 transshipment countries represent designations that trigger a license requirement under the EAR, such as Specially Designated Global Terrorist and Nonproliferation and Weapons of Mass Destruction.

entities from transshipment countries, to the Watch Lists.[24] According to State and Commerce, officials check all names on every export license application against their Watch Lists. As of September 2011, State's Watch List contained 100,248 entities, of which 8,731 (about 9 percent) were from the 13 transshipment countries we reviewed. As of November 2011, the Commerce Watch List contained 36,849 active entities, of which 8,309 (about 23 percent) were from the 13 transshipment countries we reviewed. Appendix IV details the numbers of entities from each transshipment country listed on State and Commerce Watch Lists for 2011. To confirm that the results of end-use checks are incorporated into the license application review process, we analyzed a random, nongeneralizable sample of 21 State end-use checks and 56 Commerce end-use checks during our site visits in Hong Kong, Singapore, and the UAE.[25] We submitted 11 unfavorable checks to State to determine the actions in response to the unfavorable determinations. State placed or updated the placement of 9 of the 11 entities identified in these unfavorable end-use checks on agency watch lists and referred 6 to State's enforcement division for possible investigation. For Commerce, according to its Watch List guidance, all companies that receive unfavorable prelicense checks or PSVs are placed on the Watch List. However, for the 26 end-use checks with unfavorable results that we submitted to Commerce, we could not confirm that Commerce placed the names of the associated entities on its Watch List.

Agencies may also conduct a prelicense check to verify the credentials of a party in advance of approving a license. A prelicense check may include a site visit to the proposed end user or consignee. Commerce and State may also seek the input of other agencies, particularly DOD, to vet transactions by reviewing end-user history and other factors.

---

[24]Commerce and State end-use checks may have favorable, unfavorable, or inconclusive results. A check is favorable when it can confirm that the end use and end user of an export are appropriate, unfavorable when it confirms that they are not, and inconclusive when it cannot confirm them, usually through an inability to conduct the check. Due to an unfavorable result, Commerce or State may take further action, such as denying a license or referring involved entities to enforcement agencies for investigation and possible penalties.

[25]GAO reviewed UAE-specific State end-use data collected for and reported in our report, *Persian Gulf: Implementation Gaps Limit the Effectiveness of End-Use Monitoring and Human Rights Vetting for U.S. Military Equipment,* GAO-12-89 (Washington, D.C.: Nov. 17, 2011).

Commerce Screens Applicants to Identify Trusted End Users for the VEU Program	Commerce screens applicants for a variety of factors, including reexport, to identify trusted end users for the VEU program.[26] The VEU is an export licensing framework that allows validated end users to receive eligible items on the Commerce Control List without a license. As of November 2011, Commerce conferred VEU status on 11 companies from 2 countries, China—one of the 13 GAO-designated transshipment countries—and India. The End-User Review Committee considers factors such as the entity's record of compliance with U.S. export controls and its willingness to host on-site reviews by U.S. government personnel to ensure program compliance.[27] Commerce also vets potential recipients of VEU authorizations with the law enforcement and intelligence communities. In addressing illicit transshipment risk, Commerce requires VEU applicants to adhere to conditions on diversion, retransfer, and reexport of specified items.
Agencies Address Illicit Transshipment Risk by Analyzing Shipping Data and Monitoring End Use of Items	To confirm exporters' and recipients' adherence to U.S. export control requirements, Commerce and State analyze shipping data and conduct end-use checks of items exported overseas. They use these activities to confirm compliance with export control requirements by verifying the end use of controlled items and by reviewing export documentation for potential violations.
Two Agencies Analyze Shipping Information to Identify Illicit Transshipments and Other Potential Violations	Both Commerce and State analyze shipping information to identify illicit transshipments and other potential violations of export control laws. The Census Bureau maintains shipping information on U.S. exports in the Automated Export System, the primary instrument for collecting export trade data. The U.S. government requires exporters to file shipping information with the system for any items subject to Commerce or State control, whether they need licenses or are eligible for exceptions.

Commerce uses data from the Automated Export System to determine exporter's compliance with the EAR on items subject to licensing requirements, select candidates for end-use checks, and target other compliance and enforcement activities. In addition, Commerce used |

---

[26]Transshipment is one form of reexport, according to Commerce regulations.

[27]In addition to administering the Entity List, the End-User Review Committee also is responsible for determining whether to add to, remove from, or otherwise amend the list of validated end users and associated eligible items set forth in the EAR.

available Automated Export System and international Customs data to develop a methodology that assesses the potential risk of illicit diversion of items on the Commerce Control List. This methodology is part of a Commerce developed Transshipment Identification Strategy that also included the publication of seven best practices for preventing diversion through transshipment points. U.S. agencies have assessed a risk of illicit transshipment from Hong Kong to mainland China, from UAE to Iran, and from China to Iran.

State also uses shipping information as part of its end-use monitoring program to identify illicit transshipments and other forms of diversion. Specifically, State officials said that they check shipping information against approved license applications for discrepancies when considering whether to initiate an end-use check and use such information to verify the exporter's use of license exemptions. For example, in fiscal year 2009, State reported reviewing 35,000 shipments to Canada made under an exemption specific to that country. As a result of that review, State reported initiating eight end-use checks to verify the credentials of end users who were listed on State's Watch List. State determined that the export in question did not result in a diversion. Like Commerce, State obtains shipping data from the Automated Export System maintained by the Census Bureau, pursuant to a Memorandum of Understanding with that organization. As the Memorandum of Understanding expired in November 2011, State and Census must complete a new Memorandum of Understanding for State to continue receiving this shipping data, according to a senior Census Bureau official. A State official stated that they continued to receive the shipping data between November 2011 and February 2012, but Census stopped providing this data, pending completion of a new Memorandum of Understanding, according to the Census Bureau official.

Commerce and State Verify End Use of Controlled Items

Commerce and State address illicit transshipment risk by verifying the end use of controlled items. Guidance for both agencies identifies illicit transshipment as a factor to consider in assessing the need for end-use checks.

Commerce's End-Use Checks for Transshipment Countries

Commerce may conduct an end-use check on any item subject to the EAR that is exported. Commerce's authority to conduct PSV checks is established in the Export Administration Act of 1979, which provides the legal and administrative basis for U.S. controls on dual-use exports and is supplemented by the EAR. According to Commerce, PSV checks strengthen assurances that exporters, shippers, importers, and end users comply with the terms of export license and licensing conditions.

Commerce conducts PSV checks to confirm that the dual-use item arrived at its destination and is being used as intended. Commerce Export Control Officers (ECO), special agents, or other U.S. government personnel visit companies overseas to meet with importers or end users in an attempt to verify the use and location of these items.

Our analysis of end-use checks, where Commerce made a favorable or unfavorable determination, indicated that Commerce focused its efforts on transshipment countries; it conducted 57 percent of 1,412 end-use checks for fiscal years 2008 to 2010 in the 13 transshipment countries we reviewed. Of these checks, 33 percent were unfavorable. Appendix V provides additional data on end-use checks for the 13 transshipment countries. The three locations where we conducted site visits—Hong Kong, Singapore, and UAE—represented about 36 percent of Commerce end-use checks conducted globally for this period and nearly 62 percent of unfavorable determinations worldwide.

To address transshipment concerns in Southeast Asia, Commerce stationed an ECO in Singapore, with regional responsibilities in Malaysia, Indonesia, Thailand, and the Philippines to conduct end-use checks, among other duties.[28] Commerce end-use check guidance indicates that ECOs should be aware of warning signals, including whether a consignee is aware of relevant restrictions to the reexport or retransfer of the item. For fiscal years 2008 through 2010, Commerce conducted 49 percent of all its end-use checks in five locations: UAE, Hong Kong, Singapore, Taiwan, and China. Moreover, Commerce determined that 62 percent of all unfavorable end-use checks for this period occurred in three of these locations: Hong Kong, the UAE, and Singapore.

Commerce also conducts a significant number of its PSVs on unlicensed exports.[29] Specifically, Commerce conducted 913, or about 56 percent, of the 1,619 checks on such transactions. Moreover, Commerce checks on unlicensed exports shipped in the 13 transshipment countries accounted

---

[28]In total, BIS has ECOs with areas of operation covering 12 of the 13 transshipment countries that we designated. Commerce has five ECOs stationed in 4 of the 13 transshipment countries that we designated—China (2), Hong Kong, Singapore, and the UAE. The ECOs in Hong Kong, Singapore, and the UAE also have regional responsibilities.

[29]For the purposes of this report, unlicensed exports include exports requiring no prior government review, including items subject to the EAR eligible for license exceptions.

for 70 percent of all such checks worldwide. Figure 1 shows the numbers of Commerce PSVs conducted on unlicensed exports in the 13 transshipment countries.

Figure 1: Total Commerce PSVs Conducted on Exports Shipped Without Prior U.S. Government Review Worldwide and in 13 Transshipment Countries, Fiscal Years 2008–2010

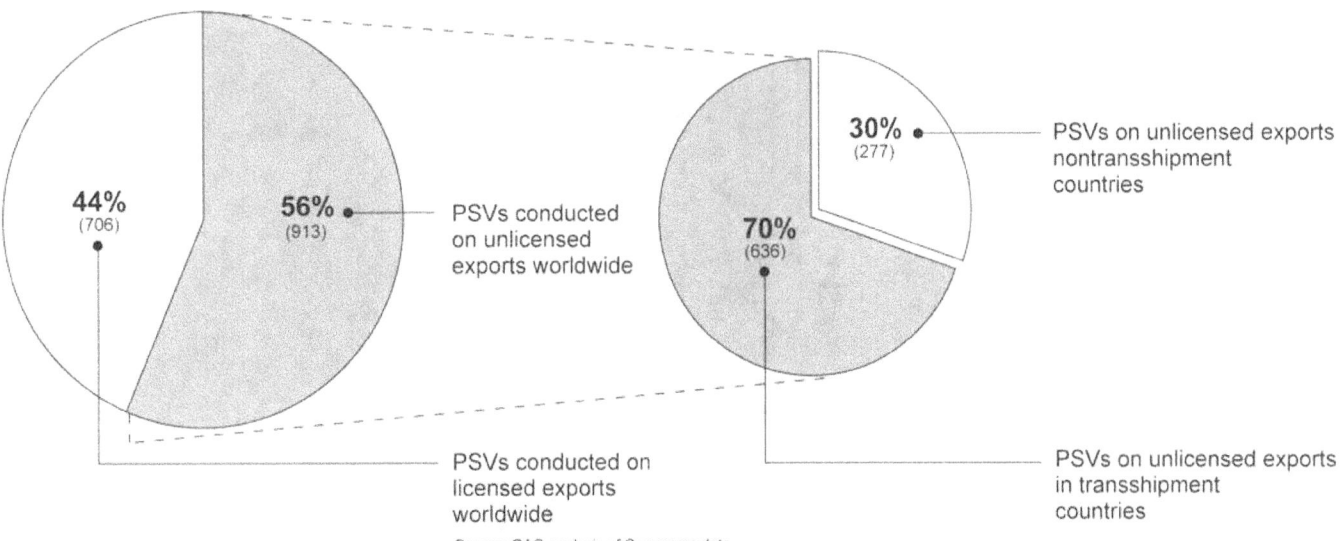

Source: GAO analysis of Commerce data.

Commerce can conduct a PSV on any exported item for any reason related to a compliance concern, such as an enforcement investigation, intelligence information, or other information that analysts have available to them. Additionally, in technical comments on a draft of this report, Commerce stated that PSVs on licensed exports are more likely to result from commodity or regional concerns, including transshipment, which will prompt further scrutiny to ultimate or intermediate consignees even though they are known not to be the end user.

Between 2008 and 2010, 223 (94 percent) of the 238 Commerce unfavorable postshipment checks in transshipment countries were on unlicensed exports. Unfavorable postshipment checks on unlicensed exports in the 13 transshipment countries accounted for 88 percent of all unfavorable postshipment checks in these countries in 2008 and rose to 97 percent in 2010. (See fig. 2.)

Figure 2: Unfavorable PSVs for Transshipment Countries, Fiscal Years 2008-2010

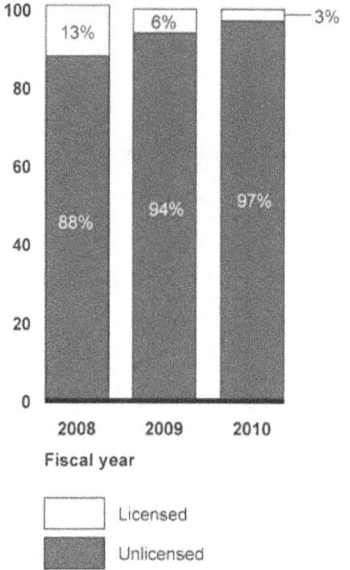

Percentage

Source: GAO analysis of Commerce data.

Note: Numbers may not add due to rounding.

Items exported without a license may pose risks to U.S. national security, according to U.S. government officials. These items include those not on the CCL and those on the CCL that do not require a license to certain destinations. For example, agencies discovered that U.S. electronics components and devices were used to build improvised explosive devices that were deployed against Coalition forces in Iraq after they were illicitly transshipped to Iran through Hong Kong. According to Commerce officials, the U.S. government established an interagency task force consisting of several defense intelligence units, and Treasury's Financial Crimes Enforcement Network, to address the threat posed by these devices.

EAR items subject to license requirements have also been transferred without a license to unauthorized destinations through transshipment points. It is the policy of the U.S. government to facilitate U.S. exports to legitimate civilian end users in the People's Republic of China (China), while preventing exports that would enhance the military capability of that country. Commerce officials stated that integrated electronic circuits have been diverted to China (a destination requiring a license for these items) through Hong Kong (where no license is required). A senior Commerce official stated that certain types of integrated electronic circuits contribute to China's military advancement.

State's End-Use Checks for Transshipment Countries

The Arms Control Export Act, as amended in 1996, requires, to the extent practicable, that end-use monitoring programs provide reasonable assurance that recipients comply with the requirements imposed by the U.S. government in the use, transfer, and security of defense articles and services.[30] In addition, end-use monitoring programs are to provide assurances that defense articles and services are used for the purposes for which they are provided. Accordingly, under State's monitoring effort known as the Blue Lantern program, State conducts end-use monitoring of direct commercial sales of defense articles and services and related technology. Specifically, a PSV is used (1) to confirm whether licensed defense goods or services exported from the United States have been received by the party named on the license and (2) to determine whether those goods have been or are being used in accordance with the provisions of that license.

Our analysis of State end-use checks under its Blue Lantern program showed that State focused a smaller portion of its end-use checks on transshipment countries than did Commerce. According to U.S. and Hong Kong government officials, the risk of illicit transshipment of dual-use exports is higher than for military exports, in part because proliferators hide their relatively small number of proliferation-related transactions—most of which involve dual-use items—within a large volume of fast-moving commercial goods. For fiscal years 2008 through 2010, State conducted 26 percent of the total number of end-use checks in the 13 transshipment countries we reviewed; 22 percent of these checks were unfavorable. In conducting end-use checks, State guidance indicates that end-use check officers are required to determine that the proposed end user appears to be a reliable recipient of sensitive U.S. defense articles, technology, or services, and that the end user is familiar with U.S. restrictions with respect to use, transfer, or reexport. See appendix V for more detailed information on Commerce and State end-use checks.

---

[30]22 U.S.C. § 2785.

Agencies Educate U.S. Exporters and Foreign Governments about Illicit Transshipment Risks, but One Program Is Largely Inactive

To educate companies and foreign governments about illicit transshipment risks, agencies have programs to review the internal controls of U.S. companies' compliance programs, conduct outreach to U.S. companies and universities, and provide training to foreign governments.

Commerce helps firms address illicit transshipment risk by conducting an informal review of firms' compliance programs at the firms' request. Commerce reviews the written procedures and internal controls for a company's compliance program against Commerce's Export Management Compliance Program guidelines to help it develop an internal control program that can thwart diversion of technologies to countries of concern. The Export Management Compliance Program guidance identifies indicators of risks posed by transshipment, such as insufficient compliance safeguards throughout the shipping process and unverified end destination addresses. In fiscal year 2010, Commerce conducted 18 reviews of corporate written compliance programs and conducted two 2-day and three 1-day seminars on developing an export management and compliance program in various U.S. cities.

Commerce and State officially have outreach programs to educate industry on issues, including illicit transshipment risks. Commerce's outreach program expanded in 2011 to increase its focus on illicit transshipment, but State's program is largely inactive. Between January and November 2011, Commerce has conducted approximately 24 outreach events across the United States. Commerce has added a training session on its *Best Practices for Preventing Unlawful Diversion of U.S. Dual-Use Items Subject to the Export Administration Regulations, Particularly through Transshipment Trade*, published in August 2011, which identifies seven best practices that guard against diversion risk, particularly through transshipment. A Commerce official stated that, due to the ongoing risk of illicit diversion of controlled items subject to the EAR, Commerce has added the best practices component to outreach events.

State's program to visit companies has been largely inactive since 2008. This program had considered transshipment risks and was in place to determine whether companies were properly exercising their regulatory responsibility in licensing and compliance. State also used the information gathered from visits to adjust or revise U.S. regulations and practices. State visited more than 60 companies between October 2005 and September 2008. While State has made two such visits since 2008, the visits were made to companies due to ongoing enforcement actions, rather than mainly for outreach.

State also addresses illicit transshipment risk by conducting export control training of foreign governments through its Export Controls and Border Security (EXBS) program. In determining the countries of focus for EXBS, State conducts country-by-country threat assessments to determine the points of greatest risk, assessing risk factors in a given country, including the risks of diversion, production, and proliferation. EXBS categorized as a diversion risk 9 of the 13 transshipment countries we examined; 7 of those countries are currently EXBS partner countries.[31] In fiscal years 2009 and 2010, EXBS conducted training in the UAE, which included a seminar on how to investigate, survey, detect, and interdict unauthorized transfers of items. EXBS announced in its 2011 Strategic Plan that transit and transshipment trade will be a priority, and EXBS will work with each shipment hub to build its capacity to target transit and transshipment cargo efficiently, without negatively affecting legitimate trade and competitiveness.

Agencies Have Not Fully Assessed Potential Impact of Control List Reforms on Resource Needs for Compliance Activities

State and Commerce have not fully assessed the potential impact of reforming the agency control lists and transferring items from State to Commerce on the resource needs of their compliance activities. Assessing impact includes analyzing the potential benefits and risks of the control list reforms, but the agencies lack information on how control list changes will impact their resource needs for conducting compliance activities. They expressed the view that some benefits would likely include a reduced compliance burden for industry and enhanced national security for the United States by focusing on items, destinations, and end users of concern. In the one assessment that it performed, Commerce estimated financial benefits of one regulatory change but did not assess any potential risks to compliance activities beyond licensing. In contrast, several compliance officials stated that risks could include the burden on Commerce's and State's capacity to monitor the end use of an increased number of items and the loss of information prior to export resulting from fewer license requirements. However, the agencies did not evaluate the implications of these risks on their resource needs.

---

[31]The seven transshipment countries that are EXBS partner countries are Indonesia, Malaysia, Philippines, Singapore, Taiwan, Thailand, and UAE.

Agencies Propose to Move Items from State to Commerce and to Introduce a New License Exception

As an interim step to creating a single control list, the administration proposed revising the list of items controlled by Commerce and State. Thus, Commerce proposed a rule in July 2011 establishing a structure to move items from the USML to the CCL that the President has determined no longer need to be controlled on that list.[32] As we previously reported, an interagency task force created export control criteria to determine the items and technologies that should be controlled by Commerce or State.[33] A DOD-led interagency team is currently revising the lists so controlled items will be identified using objective criteria such as horsepower, speed, and accuracy rather than maintaining an item on the USML simply because, historically, its form and fit has associated it with a military item. Those items that do not remain on the USML after this review will move to Commerce's jurisdiction. As of January 2012, State has proposed revisions to 5 of 20 categories of military items. The 5 categories include items such as tanks, aircraft, and submersible vessels. Proposed revisions to 4 of the 5 USML categories would change the USML controls on generic parts, components, accessories, and attachments that are specifically designed or modified for a defense article to control specific types of parts, components, accessories, and attachments.[34] Items whose functions provide immediate tactical utility without modification will remain on the USML, while all other items would move to the CCL.

Those items moved to the CCL may also become eligible for export for ultimate government end use to the destinations identified on a new license exception known as the Strategic Trade Authorization (STA). In

---

[32]76 *Fed. Reg.* 41,958 (July 15, 2011). Before the President may make such jurisdictional changes, however, he must report the results of the review to Congress. 22 U.S.C. § 2778(f)(1). The President must describe how items moved from the ITAR will be controlled under other provisions of law. The purpose of the proposed rule is to describe how items that no longer warrant control on the USML will be controlled on the CCL. 76 Fed. Reg. 76,072 (Dec. 6, 2011).

[33]GAO-11-135R.

[34]These categories include Category VII, Tanks and Military Vehicles; Category VIII, Aircraft and Associated Equipment; Category XX, Submersible Vessels Oceanographic, and Associated Equipment; Category VI, Surface Vessels of War and Special Naval Equipment. See 76 *Fed. Reg.* 41,958 (July 15, 2011); 76 *Fed. Reg.* 68,675 (Nov. 7, 2011); 76 *Fed. Reg.* 80,291 (Dec. 23, 2011); 76 *Fed. Reg.* 80,282 (Dec. 23, 2011); 76 *Fed. Reg.* 76,085 (Dec. 6, 2011); 76 Fed. Reg. 76,072. The administration also proposed the creation of a new category for gas turbine engines that would combine parts of multiple categories. 76 *Fed.Reg.*76, 072 (Dec. 6, 2011). For submersible vessels, the administration determined that most parts and components would remain on the USML because they provide a critical military and technological advantage to the United States.

June 2011, Commerce finalized this new license exception to allow exports of certain items without a license to countries determined to be low risk.[35] These items would be subject to certain notification requirements. Specifically, the STA authorizes certain exports that Commerce now controls for multiple reasons to 36 destinations, many of which are NATO allies or export control regime participants.[36] Further, the exception authorizes certain exports to an additional eight countries but limits the exception for items that Commerce now controls for national security reasons only.[37] These countries include four transshipment countries that we reviewed, Hong Kong, Singapore, Malta, and Taiwan. The licensing exception imposes additional requirements, such as directing the exporter, reexporter, or transferor to exchange information with the recipient regarding the applicable control list category number, and stating that the export occurs under the STA exception to mitigate the risk of reexport to an unauthorized destination or end user.

---

[35] 76 *Fed. Reg.* 35,276 (June 16, 2011). A license exception is an authorization that allows a company to export, under stated conditions, items subject to the EAR that would otherwise require a license.

[36] 15 C.F.R. § 740.20. Commerce authorizes exports that are controlled for specific reasons to 36 countries: Argentina, Australia, Austria, Belgium, Bulgaria, Canada, Croatia, Czech Republic, Denmark, Estonia, Finland, France, Germany, Greece, Hungary, Iceland, Ireland, Italy, Japan, Latvia, Lithuania, Luxembourg, Netherlands, New Zealand, Norway, Poland, Portugal, Romania, Slovakia, Slovenia, South Korea, Spain, Sweden, Switzerland, Turkey, and the United Kingdom.

[37] The eight destinations to which the license exception authorizes exports controlled for National Security reasons are Albania, Hong Kong, India, Israel, Malta, Singapore, South Africa, and Taiwan. According to technical comments provided by Commerce, the use of the exception is limited to those items that the Wassenaar Arrangement, a multilateral export control regime that aims to restrict trade in dual-use technologies, considers less sensitive.

Agencies Have Not Fully Assessed Potential Impact of Control List Reforms on All Compliance Activities but Have Assessed the Estimated Resource Impact on License Review

U.S. agencies have not fully assessed the potential impact that export control reform of control lists might pose for the resource needs of the range of compliance activities agencies undertake, as suggested by federal internal control standards and executive branch requirements.[38] State and Treasury officials confirmed that they have not conducted such an assessment. In technical comments on a draft of this report, Commerce stated that it had conducted an assessment of compliance activities and that it is hiring eight dedicated compliance officers. However, Commerce provided no evidence of such an assessment. Moreover, Commerce's fiscal year 2013 Congressional Budget Justification did not identify the need for compliance officers in its request for 24 additional licensing officers. Although the administration intends to move up to 30,000 license applications from State's to Commerce's jurisdiction, Commerce is targeting only 850 end-use checks in each of fiscal years 2013 and 2014, the same number it targeted for fiscal year 2012. Federal standards call for, among other things, a regulatory analysis to include the following three basic elements: (1) a statement of the need for the proposed action, (2) an examination of alternative approaches, and (3) an evaluation of the benefits and costs—quantitative and qualitative—of the proposed action and the main alternatives identified by the action. The evaluation of benefits and costs is to be informed by a risk assessment. In November 2011, Commerce' s Inspector General identified Commerce's need to ensure adequate resources to monitor compliance and to detect and prevent diversions of controlled technology in the context of export control reform as among its top management challenges for fiscal year 2012.[39]

Risk assessment is one of five standards for an internal control system that provides reasonable assurance that an organization will achieve effective and efficient operations, reliable financial reporting, and compliance with applicable laws and regulations. Commerce has not

---

[38]GAO, *Standards for Internal Control in the Federal Government*, GAO/AIMD-00-21.3.1. (Washington, D.C.: November 1999). The five standards for internal control are: control environment, risk assessment, control activities, information and communications, and monitoring. Also see GAO, *Transportation Worker Identification Credential: Internal Control Weaknesses Need to Be Corrected to Help Achieve Security Objectives*, GAO-11-657 (Washington, D.C.: May 10, 2011); OMB, Circular No. A-94,*Guidelines and Discount Rates for Benefit-Cost Analysis of Federal Programs* (Washington, D.C.: October 1992); OMB, Circular No. A-4, *Regulatory Analysis* (Washington, D.C.: September 2003).

[39]See Department of Commerce: Fiscal Year 2011 *Performance and Accountability Report,* Appendix E.

analyzed the impact of the reform on its compliance activities beyond estimating the number of State licenses that will move to its jurisdiction and potential resources needed to address them. State also has not assessed the risks of reform proposals on its compliance activities. According to a State official, current export control reform efforts are focused on revising the USML. The State official noted that, as items are moved from the USML to the CCL, the department will have better insight into potential impacts and will be able to assess resource needs.

Agencies have stated some potential benefits for national security and for exporters as a result of reform. However, agencies did not provide an analysis supporting the expected benefits. According to agencies' statements, the U.S. government would

- have greater interoperability with NATO and other allies;

- be able to focus its resources on sensitive technologies, destinations, and end users of higher risk than those found in NATO counterparts or other allies; and

- benefit from an enhanced defense industrial base by reducing the current incentives for foreign companies to avoid U.S. parts and components.

State and Commerce documents identify the following four potential advantages to industry of moving items from the USML to the CCL:

- relief from more stringent USML requirements, such as registration fees and the need to obtain manufacturing and technical assistance agreements;

- reduction of license requirements;

- simplification of license application procedures; and

- increased availability of exceptions.[40]

---

[40]According to Commerce, the USML, with few exceptions, allows exemptions from licensing requirements only to Canada. Under the rule proposed on November 7, 2011, many exports and reexports of the USML Category VII parts and components that would be moved to the CCL would become eligible for license exceptions that apply to shipments to U.S. government agencies, shipments valued at less than $1,500, parts and components being exported for use as replacement parts, temporary exports, and License Exception STA, reducing the number of licenses that exporters of these items would need.

Commerce assessed the potential impact of control list reform on its resources only for the compliance activity of license application review. Commerce documents indicate that, as of July 2011, it did not have the workforce in place to accommodate the 16,000 to 30,000 additional license applications estimated to result from the move of a significant number of items from the USML to the CCL without causing backlogs and delays. In March 2012, Commerce established a new office to adjudicate license applications and conduct other actions for items moved from the USML, and it has begun to solicit applicants to staff the office.[41] Furthermore, according to a Commerce cost benefit analysis, the new STA license exception would help remove the burdens associated with applying for a license and reduce the uncertainty associated with the license application review process. Commerce's Bureau of Industry and Security (BIS) estimated that approximately 2,300 licensed transactions would have been eligible for the STA exception in 2010. Therefore, BIS estimated that the public benefit to foregoing the license application review for those transactions eligible for the STA exception could result in a savings ranging from $1.5 million to $5.1 million per year.[42] BIS also stated that the license exception would reduce uncertainty by removing the need for U.S. exporters to inform prospective buyers of U.S. technology that sales are contingent upon government approval for each transaction. BIS also estimated that the license exception would benefit the government by allowing Commerce to focus its licensing resources on transactions of greater risk than those eligible for the STA exception. BIS officials stated that the STA exception would not increase costs to the government.

---

[41]Commerce also reprogrammed funds from both within BIS and from the Census Bureau to staff the new office.

[42]BIS calculated a range of $1.5 million to $5.2 million in potential savings to exporters by estimating several scenarios that made different assumptions about key factors such as interest rates and the face value of the licenses. The benefits of the STA exception might be even greater if Commerce included in its estimates the approximately 20,000 transactions that would be eligible for the exception once items moved from the USML to the CCL.

Agency Officials Identified Two Potential Risks of Reform for Compliance Activities, but Agencies Have Not Assessed Implications of These Risks on Resource Needs

Although U.S. agencies have not fully assessed the risks and resource implications that reform of export control lists may present in implementing compliance activities, agency officials conducting those activities identified two potential risks. These include an increased workload at Commerce from the transfer of thousands of license applications from State's to Commerce's jurisdiction, as well as the loss of information from the licensing process prior to export. Neither Commerce nor State has conducted a detailed risk assessment of the impact of the reforms on any of the compliance activities they undertake besides licensing and their associated workforce needs. *Standards for Internal Control in the Federal Government* indicates that internal controls should provide for an assessment of the external and internal risks the agency faces and that management needs to address.

A Commerce official also stated that a reduction in exports needing licenses would likely make compliance activities, such as end-use monitoring, more difficult because officials use export licenses for some of the information they rely on. Without such information, U.S. officials conducting end-use checks might need to expend more time and resources obtaining the needed information, according to the official. In fact, Commerce has focused more end-use checks on unlicensed items. We found that unlicensed exports may also pose resource implications for compliance activities concerning specific transshipment countries—Hong Kong, Singapore, and Taiwan. Items exported to these countries might be eligible to use a license exception for certain controlled items. Thus, some exports would avoid the need for prior government approval for each transaction. Commerce officials said that they might mitigate any risks that this might pose by shifting resources to target and increase compliance actions, such as outreach and shipping data analysis. In technical comments on a draft of this report, Commerce stated that it conducts end-use checks on unlicensed items now without significant difficulty and does not understand the basis for the conclusion that unlicensed exports may also pose resource implications for compliance activities concerning specific transshipment countries. However, BIS reported as recently as 2011 that it is considering requiring exporters to include additional information in the Automated Export System for unlicensed exports. Requiring this information, according to BIS, would allow it to determine more quickly the accuracy of a claimed use of authority to ship without a license or pursuant to a license exception, in some transactions. In addition, this information would enable BIS to target its end use checks of exports more effectively because it could select items of the greatest significance without extensive follow-up information from the exporter. By taking advantage of the additional information, BIS indicated that it could make more effective use of its enforcement resources.

A State compliance official said that losing the information generated by license applications would make tracking entities and commodities that are at risk more difficult and resource intensive. State officials also noted that, if reform resulted in the removal of some license requirements for certain goods, then State would need to shift its emphasis on reviewing license application data to reviewing shipping data. Currently, most defense items require a license for export. However, in certain instances, arms may be exported without a license (i.e., under an exemption) but are still subject to the Arms Export Control Act. Fewer license requirements would mean that more compliance verification would need to be conducted after the item has shipped, thereby increasing the need for PSVs, according to the official.

Conclusions

U.S. export control agencies generally address illicit transshipment risk in implementing their compliance activities, and Commerce, in particular, has focused on this risk by performing increased end-use checks in transshipment countries and on excepted or unlicensed items. Moreover, several of the agencies' compliance activities are interdependent. For example, the results of unfavorable postshipment verifications provide entity names for agencies to add to the sanctions and Watch Lists, and Watch Lists provide names that should be flagged for further scrutiny during the license review process. Therefore, changes that affect one compliance activity may also affect others. Despite this interdependence of compliance activities, agencies have not fully assessed the potential impact of the reform initiative that licensing and control list reforms may pose for resource needs. The administration's framework to reform U.S. export controls, with initial changes to Commerce and State control lists, may significantly affect the entire export control system. Moving numbers of items from State's control list to Commerce's list will shift the licensing burden for addressing concerns over misuse or diversion of these items in such countries from one agency to another. Moreover, control list reform may also shift the burden among various compliance activities in ways that cannot be anticipated without assessing the impact on resources of such changes for each activity.

Recommendations for Executive Action

As the administration moves forward with its control list reforms, we recommend that the Secretaries of Commerce and State, in consultation with other relevant agencies, assess and report on the potential impact, including the benefits and risks of proposed export control list reforms, on the resource needs of their compliance activities, particularly end-use monitoring.

Agency Comments and Our Evaluation

We provided a draft of this report to Commerce, DOD, State, and Treasury for their review and comment. Both Commerce and State provided written comments, which we have reprinted in appendixes VI and VII, respectively.[43] DOD and Treasury did not provide comments on the draft. Commerce and State also provided technical comments, which we incorporated in this report, as appropriate.

Commerce and State agreed with our recommendation to assess and report on the potential impact of export control list reforms on the resource needs of their compliance activities. State said that it will be in a better position to evaluate the resource needs for compliance activities, to include end-use monitoring, as decisions are made on moving items from the USML to the CCL. It stated that its intent to dedicate all necessary resources to compliance activities commensurate with the requirements of a revised USML remains unchanged.

Commerce stated that, to the extent that information is available, BIS has used licensing data, public comments, and interagency expertise to address both benefits and risks of moving items from the USML to CCL. However, Commerce provided no evidence that it completed such an assessment or that it assessed the benefits and risks of control list reform changes on the range of other compliance activities discussed in this report. Nonetheless, the availability of such information shows that such an assessment can be done.

Commerce also stated that several references throughout this report refer to the USML as "more stringent" and state that the CCL "imposes fewer requirements than State's controls." Commerce said it would be more accurate to say that the CCL's flexibility provides more options in

---

[43]These written comments apply to both the earlier report issued March 14, 2012, which contained information designated "For Official Use Only" and to this report.

protecting national security interests. However, State reported in its August 2011 *Final Plan for Retrospective Analysis of Existing Rules* that defense articles that do not require the stringent controls of the Arms Export Control Act will be moved to the jurisdiction of Commerce, where the licensing burden on exports can be dramatically reduced. Also, we reported in 2008 that, in most cases, Commerce's controls over dual-use items are less restrictive than State's controls over arms.[44] Many items controlled by Commerce do not require licenses for export to most destinations, while State-controlled items generally require licenses for most destinations. Also, some sanctions and embargoes only apply to items on State's U.S. Munitions List and not to those on the CCL.

We are sending copies of this report to the appropriate congressional committees; the Secretaries of Commerce, Defense, State, and the Treasury; and other interested parties. In addition, the report is available at no charge on the GAO website at http://www.gao.gov.

If you or your staff members have any questions about this report, please contact me at (202) 512-9601 or at melitot@gao.gov. Contact points for our offices of Congressional Relations and Public Affairs may be found on the last page of this report. GAO staff who made key contributions to this report are listed in appendix VIII.

Thomas Melito
Director, International Affairs and Trade

---

[44]GAO, *Export Controls: State and Commerce Have Not Taken Basic Steps to Better Ensure U.S. Interests Are Protected*, GAO-08-710T (Washington, D.C.: Apr. 24, 2008).

Appendix I: Scope and Methodology

In this review, we (1) examined how U.S. agencies use compliance activities to address the risk of illicit transshipment and (2) analyzed the extent to which U.S. agencies assessed the impact of the export control reform on the resource needs of compliance activities. Commerce provided us with transshipment-related information that it controls as being "For Official Use Only." We have not included that sensitive information in this report but have instead incorporated it into a "For Official Use Only" report that is not publicly available. To examine how U.S. agencies use compliance activities to address the risk of illicit transshipment, we reviewed documents from the Departments of Commerce, State, the Treasury, and Defense, including guidance, staffing information, and Congressional Budget Justifications. We also interviewed officials at each agency. We then identified examples of cases for each compliance activity where agency documents or officials indicated that they implemented the compliance activity to address illicit transshipment risk. We also analyzed available data, including licensing statistics, numbers of end-use checks for 13 transshipment countries, numbers of designations on various lists for entities from the 13 GAO-designated transshipment countries, numbers of 13 transshipment countries that are partner countries for Export Control and Related Border Security program training, Department of Commerce correspondence to Validated End-User designees, and agency outreach materials for companies. We also reviewed relevant laws and regulations, interviewed U.S. and host country officials, and analyzed end-use monitoring and licensing data. To identify 13 transshipment countries, we examined prior GAO work on transshipment and external diversion; congressional testimony; countries with a Commerce Export Control Officer in place; input from the Departments of State, Commerce, Justice, and Homeland Security; countries with entities on either the Entity List or Unverified List; and a listing of the world's busiest transshipment ports. We interviewed host government officials in Hong Kong and Singapore to obtain information on joint efforts with the U.S. government to mitigate illicit transshipment risks.

In examining the end-use monitoring compliance activity, we reviewed Departments of State and Commerce end-use monitoring activities through reviewing relevant program guidance, including State's Blue Lantern Guidebook, and cables associated with selected end-use checks. We interviewed officials in State's Directorate of Defense Trade Controls who administer the Blue Lantern program and reviewed export licenses. We also traveled to Singapore, Hong Kong, and the United Arab Emirates (UAE) to interview Blue Lantern points of contact and Commerce Export Control Officers. In examining State and Commerce end-use checks, we conducted an analysis of global end-use check data for fiscal years 2008–2010 and data on those checks conducted in transshipment countries. We also reviewed a random, nongeneralizable sample of end-use checks records during our overseas visits to Hong Kong, Singapore, and UAE, during which we obtained information from State and Commerce officials on how they conduct end-use checks. We reviewed 21 State Blue Lantern end-use checks from fiscal year 2009 and 2010 in Hong Kong and Singapore. Twelve of these 21 checks resulted in unfavorable determinations, and we confirmed that actions had been taken in 11 of those cases. For State end-use checks in UAE, we relied on a related GAO engagement (GAO-12-89) that reviewed State end-use monitoring in the UAE among other countries.[1] We reviewed 56 Commerce end-use checks from fiscal year 2009 through the third quarter of 2011 in Hong Kong, Singapore, and UAE.[2] We also examined the parties on the State and Commerce Watch Lists that were from the 13 transshipment countries we reviewed.

We determined that the licensing data, end-use check data, and Watch List data were sufficiently reliable for the purpose of describing how U.S. agencies use compliance activities to address the risk of illicit transshipment. For the Departments of State and Commerce licensing data, we interviewed knowledgeable agency officials in coordination with other ongoing GAO reviews of export controls. We also reviewed technical manuals related to both departments' licensing databases and determined that they were both sufficiently reliable for us to report overall statistics for how many licenses were issued for fiscal years 2009 and 2010, around the world, and for the number of licenses issued in this time period for transshipment countries. For end-use monitoring data, we also interviewed agency officials, consulted agency manuals, and compared the number of checks we received with data published by the agency. We determined that the end-use check information provided by the agency was reliable for the purposes of describing how agencies monitor the end-use of items to address the risk of illicit transshipment. For State and

---

[1] GAO-12-89.

[2] In drawing our sample of Commerce end-use checks, we considered an additional fiscal year, fiscal year 2011, as two Commerce officials responsible for conducting end-use checks in Singapore and UAE had arrived during that time, and we wanted to learn about the checks they conducted. Our sample of Commerce checks reflects a range of fiscal years, the type of checks that were conducted, and the actions that resulted from the checks.

Commerce Watch List data, we interviewed agency officials about the sources of information they incorporate into the Watch List and reviewed the guidance agencies use in updating the Watch List. We determined that the data was sufficiently reliable for the purpose of describing how agencies monitor the end-use of items to address the risk of illicit transshipment.

To analyze the extent to which agencies assessed the potential impact of the export control reform initiative for the resource needs of compliance activities, we reviewed the proposed export control reform initiatives, White House press releases on the export reform initiatives, relevant executive orders, *Federal Register* notices, comments from the public, relevant laws and regulations, and agency documentation and studies on the proposed impact of the reform initiative on their compliance activities. We interviewed agency officials and interagency and export control reform task force members to gather information on the proposed reform initiatives and agency assessments of the benefits and risks posed by those initiatives. To gather industry input into the potential impact of proposed Export Control Reform initiatives, we met with industry representatives from: (1) The Aerospace Industry Association, (2) The National Council on International Trade Development, (3) The National Association of Manufacturers, and (4) the American Chamber of Commerce in Singapore.

We conducted this performance audit from August 2010 to April 2012 in accordance with generally accepted government auditing standards. These standards require that we plan and perform the audit to obtain sufficient, appropriate evidence to provide a reasonable basis for our findings and conclusions based on our audit objectives. We believe that the evidence obtained provides a reasonable basis for our findings and conclusions based on our audit objectives.

Appendix II: Descriptions of Compliance Activities

Compliance activities provide information for exporters, licensing officials, and enforcement agencies to assess the validity of particular export transactions or to identify potential violations or prevent them before they occur. We identified eight export control compliance activities that the Departments of Commerce, State, and Treasury conduct to encourage compliance with export control laws and to prevent the diversion or misuse of exported items against U.S. allies or interests. Table 2 identifies and describes those eight compliance activities that are relevant to transshipment.

Table 2: Descriptions of Compliance Activities

Compliance activity	Description
License application review	When deciding whether to approve or deny an export license application, State and Commerce evaluate it against several factors, including an assessment of all parties to the transaction and how the recipient plans to use the item.
End-use monitoring	Prelicense or postshipment checks, including visits, to verify the bona fides of entities and appropriate receipt and use of controlled items.
Shipping data analysis	Review of selected Shippers Export Declarations to identify Export Administration Regulation violations and refer them to the Office of Export Enforcement for further investigation.
Training	A program of education, seminars, and workshops designed to help countries develop and improve their strategic trade and related border control systems.
Compliance program reviews	Reviews and critiques of companies' programs to manage export-related decisions and transactions to ensure compliance with the Export Administration Regulations and license conditions.
List maintenance	Lists that inform the licensing process by providing key information on entities of concern to licensing officers and the public.
Outreach	Courses, workshops, seminars, visits for exporters to inform them of their responsibilities to comply with export control laws and regulations.
Validated end-user assessments	Licensing framework that allows select screened end users to receive controlled items without a license.

Sources: GAO analysis of Commerce, State, and Treasury data.

Appendix III: License Application Review

When deciding whether to approve or deny an export license application, the Departments of State and Commerce evaluate it against several factors, including an assessment of all parties to the transaction and how the recipient plans to use the item. Table 3 shows the total number of Commerce and State license applications for fiscal years 2008 through 2010 worldwide and for the 13 transshipment countries that we reviewed, as well as their status for this period.

Table 3: Number of License Applications for Commerce and State for 13 Transshipment Countries, Fiscal Years 2008–2010

Agency	Location	Number of license applications	Number approved	Number denied	Number returned without action
Commerce	Worldwide	63,304	53,051	435	9,818
	Transshipment	19,693	16,596	170	2,927
State	Worldwide	164,998	82,902	865	20,319
	Transshipment	28,550	10,127	232	3,767

Sources: GAO analysis of Commerce and State data.

Appendix IV: List Maintenance

U.S. export control agencies maintain lists that inform the licensing process by providing key information on entities of concern to licensing officers and the public. The top three locations with the most entities of concern, in order, were China, the UAE, and Hong Kong for the State Watch List and China, Hong Kong, and UAE for the Commerce Watch List. Figure 3 shows the numbers of parties on State's and Commerce's Watch Lists from the 13 transshipment countries that we reviewed. As of September 2011, State's Watch List contained 100,248 parties, of which 8,731 (about 9 percent) were from the 13 transshipment countries we reviewed. As of December 2011, the Commerce Watch List contained 36,849 active entities, of which 8,309 (about 23 percent) were from the 13 transshipment countries we reviewed.

Figure 3: Numbers of Parties on State and Commerce Watch List by Transshipment Country for 2011

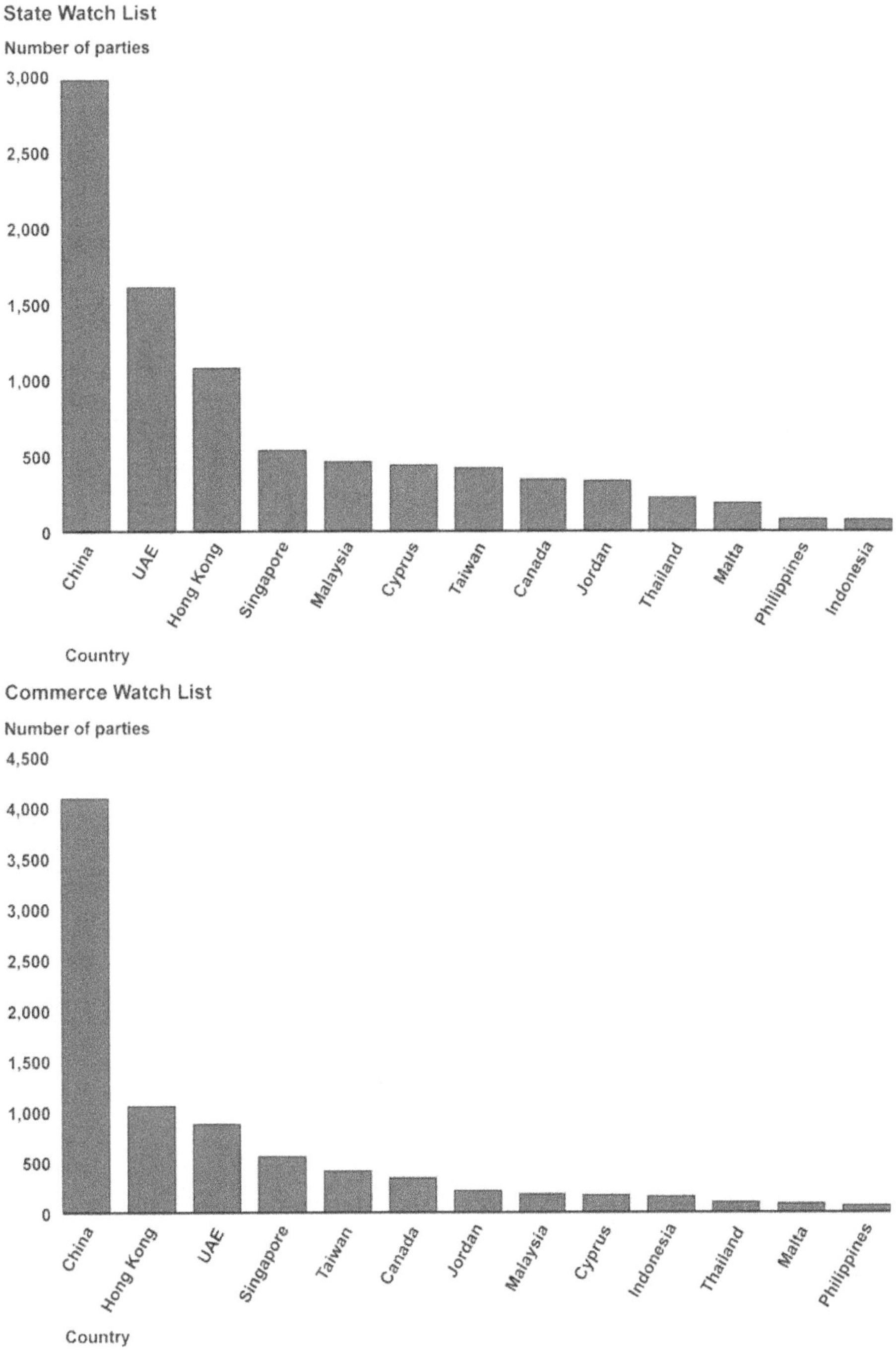

State Watch List

Commerce Watch List

Sources: GAO analysis of State and Commerce data.

Our analysis of the Department of Commerce's end-use checks shows that Commerce focused its efforts on transshipment countries; it conducted 57 percent of all end-use checks for fiscal years 2008 to 2010 in the 13 transshipment countries we reviewed. Of these checks, 33 percent were unfavorable. In contrast, the Department of State conducted 26 percent of all end-use checks for fiscal years 2008 to 2010 in the 13 transshipment countries we reviewed. Table 4 shows end-use checks for Commerce and State for the 13 transshipment countries and worldwide for fiscal years 2008-2010.

Table 4: Commerce and State End-Use Checks, Fiscal Years 2008–2010

Fiscal year	Total-worldwide Commerce	Total-worldwide State	Checks-transshipment countries Commerce	Checks-transshipment countries State	Percentage of checks in transshipment countries Commerce	Percentage of checks in transshipment countries State
2008	376	543	197	158	52 %	29 %
2009	547	649	317	156	58 %	24 %
2010	489	723	290	178	59 %	25 %
Total	**1,412**	**1,915**	**804**	**492**	**57 %**	**26 %**

Source: GAO analysis of Commerce and State data.

For fiscal years 2008 through 2010, Commerce conducted about 57 percent of the total number of end-use checks in the 13 transshipment countries we reviewed. (See fig. 4.)

Figure 4: Commerce's End-Use Checks in 13 Transshipment Countries, Fiscal Years 2008–2010

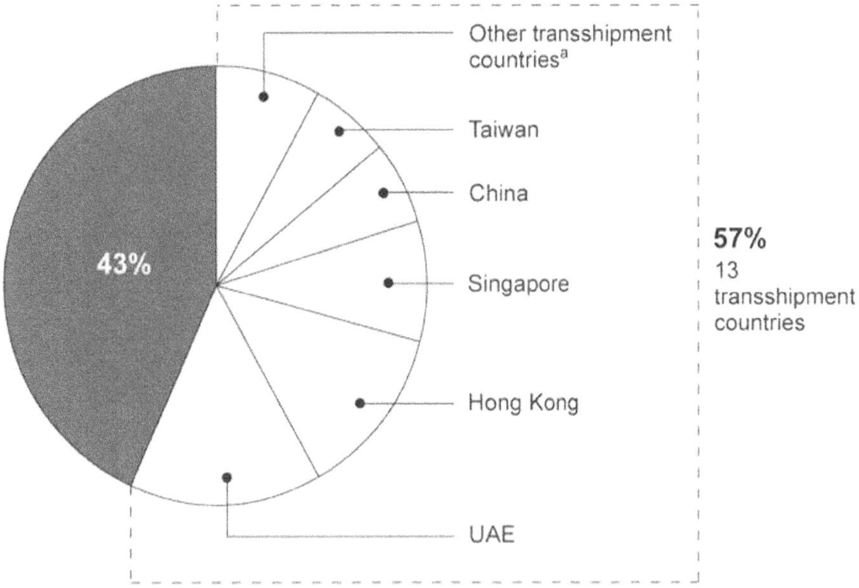

Source: GAO analysis of Commerce end-use check data.

Note: This figure represents only completed prelicense and postshipment verifications for 2008 through 2010.

[a]Other transshipment countries include: Malta, Canada, Cyprus, Philippines, Jordan, Indonesia, Thailand, Malaysia.

For fiscal years 2008 through 2010, State conducted about 26 percent of the total number of end-use checks in the 13 transshipment countries we reviewed; 22 percent of these checks were unfavorable (see fig. 5).

Figure 5: State's Blue Lantern End-Use Checks in 13 Transshipment Countries, Fiscal Years 2008–2010

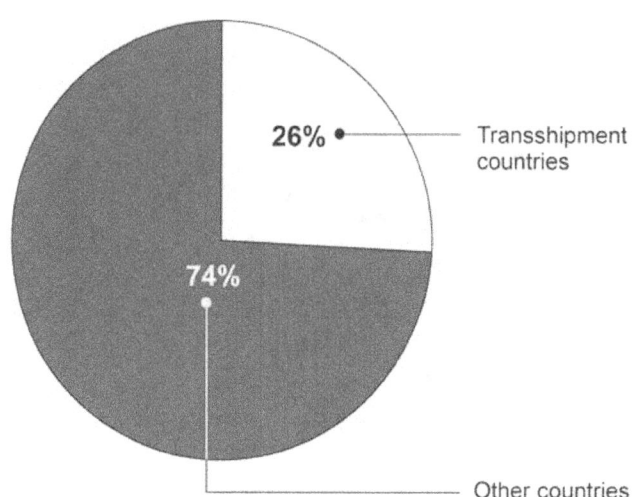

Source: GAO analysis of State data.

Appendix VI: Comments from the Department of Commerce

Note: GAO comments supplementing those in the report text appear at the end of this appendix.

UNITED STATES DEPARTMENT OF COMMERCE
The Secretary of Commerce
Washington, D.C. 20230

March 9, 2012

Mr. Thomas Melito
Director, International Affairs and Trade
Government Accountability Office
441 G Street, NW
Washington, DC 20548

Dear Mr. Melito:

Thank you for the opportunity to comment on the draft report entitled, "Agencies Need to Assess Reform's Impact on Compliance Activities" GAO-12-394SU.

The Department of Commerce concurs with the recommendation made to the Secretaries of Commerce and State. As noted in more detail in the attached comments, the Bureau of Industry and Security continues to update assessments of both potential licensing volume and resources needed to help ensure exporter compliance with the proposed controls on items to be moved from the United States Munitions List to the Commerce Control List.

If you have any questions, please contact Mark Crace in the Office of Administration at (202) 482-8093 or via e-mail at mark.crace@bis.doc.gov.

Sincerely,

John E. Bryson

GAO-12-394SU
EXPORT CONTROL:
Agencies Need to Assess Reform's Impact on Compliance Activities

Recommendation:
1) Secretaries of Commerce and State, in consultation with other relevant agencies, assess
   and report on the potential impact, including the benefits and risks of proposed export
   control list reforms on the resource needs of their compliance activities, particularly
   end-use monitoring.

The Bureau of Industry and Security (BIS) General Comments
- To address the increased volume, BIS has created a Munitions Control Division (MCD)
  within the Office of Strategic Industries and Economic Security to process license
  applications, and conduct compliance activities, for items proposed to be moved to the
  Commerce Control List's (CCL) new "600 series" from the United States Munitions List
  (USML). MCD will have a staff of 24.

- MCD will have eight compliance specialists who will work within the organization to
  monitor items shipped. These compliance specialists will work side-by-side with
  enforcement analysts to identify entities at which to conduct both end-use checks overseas
  and U.S. company onsite audits.

- In addition, BIS is developing a new outreach and education model to address the new
  control structure. This model will go beyond existing outreach strategies to attract a large
  number of stakeholders who have traditionally received licenses from the Department of
  State, including defense contractors and exporters, manufacturers, distributors, logistics and
  related transporters, and small and medium sized corporations who have had limited
  involvement in dual-use exporting.

- To the extent that information is available, BIS has used licensing data, public comments and
  interagency expertise to address both benefits and risks of moving items from the USML to
  CCL. The benefits include moving less sensitive munitions items, mostly parts and
  components, to a more flexible licensing regime, thus treating the export of tanks differently
  than the tank wheel-nut.

- There are several references throughout the document, including on the first page and on
  page 22, in which the GAO refers to the USML as "more stringent" and states that the CCL
  "imposes fewer requirements than State's controls." It would be more accurate to say that
  the CCL provides more flexibility than the USML because it provides more options in
  protecting national security interests.

Following are GAO's comments on the Department of Commerce's letter
dated March 9, 2012.

GAO Comments

1. Commerce stated that its new Munitions Control Division will include
   24 personnel; eight of these 24 will be compliance specialists who will
   work within the organization to monitor items shipped. These
   compliance specialists will work with enforcement analysts to identify
   entities to conduct both end-use checks overseas and U.S. company
   onsite audits. However, the rationale for these eight compliance
   specialists is unclear. Commerce's fiscal year 2013 budget request
   listed only 24 licensing officers and Commerce did not provide us with
   any analysis to show that these would include specifically 8
   compliance specialists. In addition, while the administration intends to
   move up to 30,000 license applications from State to Commerce's
   jurisdiction, Commerce is targeting only 850 end-use checks for each
   fiscal year 2013 and 2014, which is the same number as for fiscal
   year 2012.

2. Commerce stated that, to the extent that information is available, BIS
   has used licensing data, public comments, and interagency expertise
   to address both benefits and risks of moving items from the USML to
   CCL. It stated that the benefits include moving less sensitive
   munitions items, mostly parts and components, to a more flexible
   licensing regime. However, Commerce provided no evidence that it
   completed an assessment of benefits and risks, nor that it assessed
   the benefits and risks of control list reform changes on the range of
   other compliance activities this report discussed. Nonetheless, the
   availability of such information shows that such an assessment can be
   done.

3. Commerce stated that our report makes several references to the
   USML as "more stringent" and that the CCL "imposes fewer
   requirements than State's controls." Commerce said it would be more
   accurate to say that the CCL's flexibility provides more options in
   protecting national security interests. However, State reported in its
   August 2011 *Final Plan for Retrospective Analysis of Existing Rules*
   that defense articles that do not require the stringent controls of the
   Arms Export Control Act will be moved to Commerce's jurisdiction,
   where the licensing burden on exports can be dramatically reduced. In
   addition, we reported in 2008 that, in most cases, Commerce's

controls over dual-use items are less restrictive than State's controls over arms.[1] Many items that Commerce controls do not require licenses for export to most destinations, while State-controlled items generally require licenses for most destinations. Also, some sanctions and embargoes only apply to items on State's USML and not to those on the CCL.

---

[1] GAO-08-710T.

Appendix VII: Comments from the Department of State

United States Department of State

Chief Financial Officer

Washington, D.C. 20520

Mr. Loren Yager
Managing Director
International Affairs and Trade
Government Accountability Office
441 G Street, N.W.
Washington, D.C. 20548-0001

MAR -2 2012

Dear Mr. Yager:

We appreciate the opportunity to review your draft report, "EXPORT CONTROLS: Agencies Need to Assess Reform's Impact on Compliance Activities," GAO Job Code 320806.

The enclosed Department of State comments are provided for incorporation with this letter as an appendix to the final report.

If you have any questions concerning this response, please contact Steven Rice, Deputy Director, Bureau of Political-Military Affairs at (202) 663-2803.

Sincerely,

James L. Millette

cc: GAO – Thomas Melito
      PM– Andrew J. Shapiro
      State/OIG – Evelyn Klemstine

<u>**Department of State Comments on GAO Draft Report**</u>

<u>**EXPORT CONTROLS: Agencies Need to Assess Reform's Impact on
Compliance Activities**</u>
(GAO 12-394SU, GAO Code 320806)

Thank you for the opportunity to comment on your draft report entitled *"Export
Controls: Agencies Need to Assess Reform's Impact on Compliance Activities."*
GAO's report recommends that the Secretaries of Commerce and State, in
consultation with other relevant agencies, assess and report on the potential impact,
including the benefits and risks of proposed export control list reforms, on the
resource needs of their compliance activities, particularly end-use monitoring.

The Department of State agrees with GAO's recommendation. As GAO points out
on page 23 of its draft report, the Department will be in a better position to
evaluate the resource needs for compliance activities, to include end-use
monitoring, as decisions are made on moving items from the U.S. Munitions List
(USML) to the Commerce Control List (CCL). Thus, our intent to dedicate all
necessary resources to compliance activities commensurate with the requirements
of a revised USML remains unchanged.

Appendix VIII: GAO Contact and Staff Acknowledgments

GAO Contact

Thomas Melito, (202) 512-9601 or melitot@gao.gov.

Staff Acknowledgments

In addition to the individual named above, key contributors to this report were Joseph A. Christoff, Director (ret.); Jeff Phillips, Assistant Director; Richard G. Howland, Analyst-in-Charge; Mason Thorpe Calhoun; Alberto Leff; Elena McGovern; and Lynn Cothern. Martin de Alteriis, Justin Fisher, Mitchell Karpman, and Hai Tran provided assistance with design and methodology, statistics, data analysis, and technical expertise, respectively. Grace Lui provided legal support, Etana Finkler provided graphics support, and Joyce Evans, Jeremy Sebest, and Cynthia S. Taylor provided assistance in editing and report preparation.

Related GAO Products

Export Controls: Proposed Reforms Create Opportunities to Address Enforcement Challenges. GAO-12-246. Washington, D.C.: March 27, 2012.

Persian Gulf: Implementation Gaps Limit the Effectiveness of End-Use Monitoring and Human Rights Vetting for U.S. Military Equipment, GAO-12-89. Washington, D.C.: November 17, 2011.

Export Controls: Improvements Needed to Prevent Unauthorized Technology Releases to Foreign Nationals in the United States. GAO-11-354. Washington, D.C.: February 2, 2011.

Defense Exports: Reporting on Exported Articles and Services Needs to Be Improved. GAO-10-952. Washington, D.C.: September 21, 2010.

Persian Gulf: U.S. Agencies Need to Improve Licensing Data and to Document Reviews of Arms Transfers for U.S. Foreign Policy and National Security Goals. GAO-10-918. Washington, D.C.: September 28, 2010.

Export Controls: Observations on Selected Countries' Systems and Proposed Treaties. GAO-10-557. Washington, D.C.: June 28, 2010.

Iran Sanctions: Complete and Timely Licensing Data Needed to Strengthen Enforcement of Export Restrictions. GAO-10-375. Washington, D.C.: March 4, 2010.

Export Controls: Challenges with Commerce's Validated End-User Program May Limit its Ability to Ensure That Semiconductor Equipment Exported to China is Used as Intended. GAO-08-1095. Washington, D.C.: October 27, 2008.

Defense Trade: State Department Needs to Conduct Assessments to Identify and Address Inefficiencies and Challenges in the Arms Export Process. GAO-08-89. Washington, D.C.: January 8, 2008.

Nonproliferation: U.S. Efforts to Combat Nuclear Networks Need Better Data on Proliferation Risks and Program Results. GAO-08-21. Washington, D.C.: October 31, 2007.

Defense Trade: Clarification and More Comprehensive Oversight of Export Exemptions Certified by DOD Are Needed. GAO-07-1103. Washington, D.C.: October 19, 2007.

Export Controls: Challenges Exist in Enforcement of an Inherently Complex System. GAO-07-265. Washington, D.C.: December 20, 2006.

Export Controls: Agencies Should Assess Vulnerabilities and Improve Guidance for Protecting Export-Controlled Information at Universities. GAO-07-70. Washington, D.C.: December 5, 2006.

Export Controls: Improvements to Commerce's Dual-Use System Needed to Ensure Protection of U.S. Interests in the Post-9/11 Environment. GAO-06-638. Washington, D.C.: June 26, 2006.

Defense Trade: Arms Export Control System in the Post-9/11 Environment. GAO-05-234. Washington, D.C.: February 16, 2005.

Nonproliferation: Improvements Needed To Better Control Technology Exports For Cruise Missiles And Unmanned Aerial Vehicles. GAO-04-175. Washington, D.C.: January 23, 2004.

Export Controls: Post-Shipment Verification Provides Limited Assurance That Dual-Use Items Are Being Properly Used. GAO-04-357. Washington, D.C.: January 12, 2004.

Defense Trade: Better Information Needed To Support Decisions Affecting Proposed Weapons Transfers. GAO-03-694. Washington, D.C.: July 11, 2003.

Nonproliferation: Strategy Needed To Strengthen Multilateral Export Control Regimes. GAO-03-43. Washington, D.C.: October 25, 2002.

Export Controls: Processes for Determining Proper Control of Defense-Related Items Needs Improvement. GAO-02-996. Washington, D.C.: September 20, 2002.

Export Controls: Department of Commerce Controls over Transfers of Technology to Foreign Nationals Need Improvement. GAO-02-972. Washington, D.C.: September 6, 2002.

Lessons to Be Learned From the Country Export Exemption. GAO-02-63. Washington, D.C.: March 29, 2002.

Export Controls: Clarification of Jurisdiction for Missile Technology Items Needed. GAO-02-120. Washington, D.C.: October 9, 2001.

GAO's Mission	The Government Accountability Office, the audit, evaluation, and investigative arm of Congress, exists to support Congress in meeting its constitutional responsibilities and to help improve the performance and accountability of the federal government for the American people. GAO examines the use of public funds; evaluates federal programs and policies; and provides analyses, recommendations, and other assistance to help Congress make informed oversight, policy, and funding decisions. GAO's commitment to good government is reflected in its core values of accountability, integrity, and reliability.
Obtaining Copies of GAO Reports and Testimony	The fastest and easiest way to obtain copies of GAO documents at no cost is through GAO's website (www.gao.gov). Each weekday afternoon, GAO posts on its website newly released reports, testimony, and correspondence. To have GAO e-mail you a list of newly posted products, go to www.gao.gov and select "E-mail Updates."
Order by Phone	The price of each GAO publication reflects GAO's actual cost of production and distribution and depends on the number of pages in the publication and whether the publication is printed in color or black and white. Pricing and ordering information is posted on GAO's website, http://www.gao.gov/ordering.htm. Place orders by calling (202) 512-6000, toll free (866) 801-7077, or TDD (202) 512-2537. Orders may be paid for using American Express, Discover Card, MasterCard, Visa, check, or money order. Call for additional information.
Connect with GAO	Connect with GAO on Facebook, Flickr, Twitter, and YouTube. Subscribe to our RSS Feeds or E-mail Updates. Listen to our Podcasts. Visit GAO on the web at www.gao.gov.
To Report Fraud, Waste, and Abuse in Federal Programs	Contact: Website: www.gao.gov/fraudnet/fraudnet.htm E-mail: fraudnet@gao.gov Automated answering system: (800) 424-5454 or (202) 512-7470
Congressional Relations	Katherine Siggerud, Managing Director, siggerudk@gao.gov, (202) 512-4400, U.S. Government Accountability Office, 441 G Street NW, Room 7125, Washington, DC 20548
Public Affairs	Chuck Young, Managing Director, youngc1@gao.gov, (202) 512-4800 U.S. Government Accountability Office, 441 G Street NW, Room 7149 Washington, DC 20548

Please Print on Recycled Paper.

www.ingramcontent.com/pod-product-compliance
Lightning Source LLC
Chambersburg PA
CBHW080908290526
45795CB00007BA/2457